I0141866

FINDING YOUR VOICE:

STRAIGHT TALK

FOR LAWYERS

FINDING YOUR VOICE: STRAIGHT TALK FOR LAWYERS

Andrea L. Colby, Esq.

PRO SE COACHING, LLC

FINDING YOUR VOICE: STRAIGHT TALK FOR LAWYERS

Copyright © 2015, Andrea L. Colby

ISBN-13: 978-0692519882

ISBN-10: 0692519882

MLilah Publishing

Pro Se Coaching, LLC

12 Woodside Avenue

Metuchen, NJ 08840

DEDICATION

This book is dedicated to my parents, Jerome and Betty Loshin, who always told me that I was capable of anything I put my mind to and challenged me to put my mind to many, many things. This book is also dedicated to my husband and son, Michael and Steven Colby, who always support me with love and understanding.

Contents

INTRODUCTION ix

LIFE WITHOUT A VOICE 1

HOW I FOUND MY OWN VOICE 11

FINDING YOUR OWN VOICE 19

FIRST STEP IN FINDING YOUR
VOICE: EXERCISE 27

WHAT'S THE NEXT STEP? 41

COACHING EXAMPLE #1:
"I'VE GOT TOO MUCH TO DO AND
TOO LITTLE TIME TO DO IT IN!" 43

COACHING EXAMPLE #2:
THEY NEVER LISTEN TO ME!!! 57

COACHING EXAMPLE #3:
WHERE DID ALL MY WORK GO? 71

ABOUT ANDREA 83

INTRODUCTION

In my years of practice as an intellectual property attorney, newer attorneys have often asked me, "What do I need to know to succeed as an attorney?" Reflecting on my own career and on the careers of all the skilled attorneys I've ever met, observed and admired, my answer is: "To succeed in the law, you must find your own true voice."

The most successful attorneys I know are those who can speak for themselves and for their clients. After all, if you have not found the voice to represent yourself, how can you possibly speak effectively for those you represent? At least, that's what the powers that be, those who are deciding your fate, are thinking! But what does "finding your voice" really mean?

- **Finding your voice requires that**

you know yourself completely: *all* your strengths, *all* your weaknesses. It means that you feel *completely* self-confident.

- **Most important, finding your voice means that you know what you don't know. And you feel comfortable asking and learning about what you don't know.**

We all hear, from the beginning of our careers, almost ***ad nauseam***, that "the law is a service profession." This means that we, as attorneys, exist professionally to help our clients navigate the legal system so they can protect themselves, plan for their futures and develop productive relationships with others. We help them tell their stories to family members, to business partners, to the court. Effective, knowledgeable communication is key to eliciting and telling those stories. Self-doubt, which stems in large part from the lack of self-knowledge, imposes a huge obstacle to expressing yourself effectively.

Self-knowledge requires you to be aware of who you are, what you know and what comes out of your mouth. It also requires that you understand how you affect the people around you: clients, colleagues and opposing counsel. Who hasn't awakened at 3 a.m., after an important presentation or meeting, reviewing everything you said or did and thinking, "Oh no! How could I have said/done *that?!*" Not a productive way to spend the wee hours of the morning!

But when you feel at ease with yourself, you don't spend so much time and energy worrying about *yourself* that you can't hear what your client needs or give them great advice. You can ask the right questions to get what you need without worrying that you will appear "silly" or "stupid." In my experience, the attorneys who are able to say, "I don't know" and ask questions with confidence are the ones who are most effective. **Because they follow up "I don't know" with "I can find out!"**

When you have found your voice, you will know how to advise your clients in a way they can hear and appreciate. You will use your voice to communicate effectively to work together with your colleagues so that they are enthusiastic about working with you. In addition, you will know how to represent yourself and your clients to the court and opposing counsel successfully. And you'll sleep through the night without revisiting and questioning every statement you made during the day.

- **Finding your voice is a process!**

This process involves looking in

the mirror and being honest with yourself about what you do well and what you need to do better. It also entails seeking, understanding and integrating feedback and striving for constant improvement. It involves preparing for *how* you give advice as well as *what* advice you give. In addition, the process includes finding the best, most efficient ways of completing your work and presenting it so that your supervisors and clients understand and appreciate your advice.

When you know that you have done a great job, and you know *why* you've done a great job, you will feel authentically self-confident, your voice will reflect that feeling and your clients and colleagues will trust you and come back again and again.

LIFE WITHOUT A VOICE

Right out of law school, I was fortunate to get a position in the patent law department of a large corporation. Although I'd graduated from engineering school and law school, I was completely naïve about how to succeed, in my job and, ultimately, in my career. At that time, and for quite some time afterward, I believed that if I worked hard and did good work, I would do well. Many newly minted law school graduates, starting out at law firms, government agencies and corporate law departments, feel the same way.

I was one of three new attorneys fresh out of law school to start at my company. One colleague, Harry, seemed to know exactly how to dress, exactly how to delegate work to our secretary, exactly what to say to our managers and how to get the best work. It struck me that he wasn't necessarily the most talented of the new attorneys, but he was treated with kid gloves.

The other new attorney and I were much less self-possessed and confident. We were fascinated with Harry and his style and often marveled at what he seemed to have that we didn't. We were just aware that we "didn't get it," but analyze as we might, we simply didn't know *how* to "get it." We knew that we were learning what we needed to learn substantively, and that we were getting the experience we needed. But somehow we both had the feeling that we were missing something. For example, all three of us shared a secretary, but she only carried out Harry's work.

Ultimately, I realized that the most frustrating part of starting out was that "I didn't know what I didn't know," either with respect to the practice of patent law or with respect to presenting myself with confidence.

Rather quickly, I realized that had I continued to stay with this company, for the foreseeable future, my job would consist of exactly what I'd been doing for the year and a half that I'd already been there. In addition, we were told that, due to the company's excessive spending on its new headquarters building out of state, we would not receive raises that year.

In view of all these issues, I decided to leave and get some law firm experience. I was under the impression that working at a law firm would give me broad legal experience as well as some of the "polish" that law firm attorneys had. I guess I had the idea that "polish" would somehow diffuse into my being through osmosis—it wasn't clear to me exactly how that would occur.

I secured a position as an associate at a midsize, well-established intellectual property boutique firm in midtown Manhattan. I was assigned a number of patent applications to draft and prosecute. The firm also assigned me to a patent litigation that had been pending for almost seven years. Again, I assumed that if I worked hard and did good work, I would be recognized and rewarded.

What I hadn't understood, however, was the political aspect of the job: there were associates who had less experience than I did but who resented the fact that my name went above theirs on the letterhead. I was shocked that some of them attempted to "delegate" to me! When a partner asked one of them to give me some patent applications to prosecute, one fellow associate took the opportunity to delegate to me tasks that he considered "scut work."

Fortunately, I had enough self-confidence and courage at the time to approach the partner and ask whether this work was what he intended to give me—he said it was not and straightened out the situation. Had I not spoken up and trusted in my own voice to express myself, I would have ended up wasting a lot of time and energy. Naturally, it didn't endear me to the other associate. But I decided to let that go and work hard on the tasks at hand. There were other instances of this type of behavior. And to some extent, it was condoned and even admired by some partners.

I, however, was criticized for being "too nice," for dressing in a feminine manner (a friend told me I shouldn't wear "party dresses" to the office, i.e., that I should wear as masculine work uniform as possible). Other associates continued to try to dump distasteful work on me. While I ultimately sought experience and was rewarded with plenty of interesting work, the hours were overwhelming: I worked evenings and weekends and had very little social life outside of the office.

I had no idea how to compete in such an environment, nor did I particularly wish to do so. I just wanted to work and get my job done. And, as typical of law firms, the partners rarely, if ever, gave constructive developmental feedback: if you did something wrong, you definitely heard about it. You assumed that if you heard nothing, you were doing okay. After a time in that environment, I lost both my self-confidence and my voice and simply did everything I was asked to do without questioning.

It's not unusual for attorneys to react badly to the stresses of working in a law firm and failing to balance work and personal life.

Many young lawyers with whom I've spoken express the feeling that they know something is wrong in their careers at a firm, but they can't say exactly what it is and they don't know how to address it. Their support systems begin to fail and the attorneys have no time or energy to strengthen them. Some attorneys turn to drink or other self-destructive behavior. Of course, it is best to learn appropriate skills early on in order to prevent this from happening.

In time, I understood that no matter what I did, how many hours I worked, how many partners with whom I worked, I would never be completely appreciated or treated with respect at the firm.

When I'd been at the firm for about three years, a recruiter called and told me, "You belong in the Law Department at XX Company, but they never hire anyone and nobody ever leaves!" "Oh well!" I thought. I had no idea what the major attraction about working in the XX Law Department might be, but I filed the advice in the back of my mind and went back to work.

About three years later, a partner came into my office to give me my review and raise and told me that they "weren't sure you'll make partner." I asked exactly what that meant—for example, was he asking me to leave the firm? He replied, "No! We really like your work! But you need to get more litigation experience."

I thought that ironic, considering that I was working on six litigations at the time. It all made very little sense to me, but I accepted the situation and decided that I would need to consider leaving, despite all the blood, sweat and tears that I'd poured into that job.

So I still didn't "get it": I had no idea why, despite my hard work and valuable work, I wasn't appreciated when other associates somehow were being brought along and tended to and recognized. And I still had no way of asking, speaking for myself and truly finding out what the issue was that prompted this review.

By coincidence, shortly after this meeting I received a call from a recruiter telling me that XX Company was looking for a patent attorney! I interviewed and received an offer. And I have spent the rest of my legal career in the XX Law Department.

HOW I FOUND MY OWN VOICE

My new job let me grow in ways that I had not been able to in my previous positions. I was grateful to have found an excellent mentor— but I still hadn't found my voice. What I didn't realize early on during the time I worked with my mentor in my new position was that this was *precisely* what he wanted me to do: to tell my clients what they *needed* to hear, rather than what they *wanted* to hear, in a clear way that came from my thorough study and intimate knowledge of a situation.

He wanted me to *know clearly* that I knew exactly what I was talking about. He also wanted me to feel confident that facts and law supported my advice. He wanted me to understand that the clients needed *all* the facts and legal input in order to make a decision, even if the facts and the law might be difficult for them to hear. But I wasn't quite ready to understand his advice at the time: I still did not have complete confidence in myself, which undermined the strength of my delivery of advice. What I needed to do was go through the process of finding my "legal self" and, consequently, my own voice.

Find out who you are and then be who you are:

I have been fortunate to work with many brilliant, skilled attorneys and, as part of the process of finding my own voice, I learned to observe closely how they interacted with clients. In that way, I could emulate them and try out different styles of expressing myself in order to find the way I felt most comfortable. Lots of trial and error is involved in this part of the process!

It was important to be able to identify great colleagues and really pay attention to exactly how they communicated. I also realized that I needed to speak up and ask them what they were doing and why they did it in order to understand how I could incorporate these learnings into my own practice.

As lawyers, our job is to support our clients: we need to be sensitive to our clients' needs and respond in an appropriate way. Whether in a corporation, where we support the business, or in private practice, lawyers must be able to *connect* with their clients to help them make the decisions that are important to them. I also discovered that each of us had to find our own way of rendering advice that is consistent with our own personalities. When we do that, clients listen!

I am a relatively soft-spoken person. I once had a supervisor who insisted that when giving tough advice, I needed to yell and bang the table. By this time, through experimentation and practice, I had developed a healthier self-esteem than I had at the law firm. I explained to him, "No, that's not who I am. I don't need to do that to be taken seriously." In fact, I knew that had I done that, my clients would have ignored my advice because it is so much at odds with who they knew me to be.

I had finally understood that I deserved to be heard as *myself*: a well-trained and intelligent attorney who has my clients' best interests at heart. Pretending to be someone or something I'm not would come across falsely to my clients. And I'd gained enough of my voice not only to express this to my supervisor but to know how best to speak with my clients. I needed to take in the criticism, evaluate it and respond to it without taking it personally.

Getting to that place is a process: I had learned to outline tough advice based on what I knew about my *audience*, not on the way I *assumed* they wanted to hear it or in the way other attorneys might have given it. I practice it, out loud, *in my own voice*, so that I find the words that come most authentically from my mouth. I do the same with communications I have with my supervisors and my peers.

Not long after this, I had occasion to render an opinion to another client. I rehearsed the major points and practiced my presentation, considering what my client needed to know. I found that doing this gave me confidence in my advice and in the delivery of my advice. I spoke simply and directly. A couple of days after I gave my advice, my client called me and said, "I really appreciated how you gave that advice; I understood everything and you gave me very clear guidelines. Just wanted to let you know. Thanks!" She had heard what I was trying to get across because I presented the advice effectively and authentically.

Are there times when we, as attorneys, need to raise our voices and pound on the table, even virtually? Yes, of course! We might be in an adversarial situation in court or in negotiations where raising our voice may be effective to support our clients. But we need to *choose* when to do that and how we will do that. We need to be *comfortable* making that choice and *aware* of when to make that choice. Becoming aware is a full process as well.

When we are faithful to our true selves and feel comfortable with how we express ourselves, others receive our communications with understanding and appreciation. By being authentic, by not being persuaded to change to fit a stereotype, even by a supervisor, we can create the integrity for us to succeed in conveying what we need to convey in our own unique voice *and be heard.*

FINDING YOUR OWN VOICE

The first step in the process of finding your own unique voice is to figure out who you are. You can begin this process with the exercise at the end of this chapter. You will explore these questions: What are your skills and talents? What do you love to do? What do you find challenging?

These are questions only *you* can answer. Answering these questions requires you to set aside time and space to think and remember what's important to you, what has always come easily to you and what is difficult. It can also be helpful to discuss your findings with an objective third party, such as a mentor or coach.

Another very important aspect of learning who you really are professionally is the answer to the following questions: How well do you know how your colleagues, supervisors and clients view you? What do they see as your best attributes? What legal and interpersonal skills do you need to work on?

One excellent way of finding out is to seek feedback, formally or informally. Many of us fear getting feedback—you probably will not be surprised to hear that, as attorneys, we tend to have large but very fragile egos! Doing excellent work is important to us and we take great pride in our output, so receiving honest comments implying that there are areas we need to work on can be difficult for us. But it can be extremely powerful if we receive feedback in an open way.

You should only explore the second part of the process after doing the summary exercise below. Then you will have a good idea of what is good about yourself before you seek third-party feedback, and you will be in a position not to let feedback hurt your feelings or become overly emotional about it.

Years ago, I received some frank but honest feedback at my job. My boss gave me some tough criticism from my clients that required me to work through some upsetting issues. My first reaction to the criticism was that they were "wrong" and that the feedback was "unfair." After this frank conversation with my boss, I spent at least twenty-four hours in bed with the covers over my head, literally and figuratively.

But then I had an epiphany. I realized that whether or not my clients were truly right or wrong didn't matter. This was their *perception*, and I needed to address why they were feeling the way they were feeling. I spent a miserable weekend berating myself, but I slowly came to realize that I had

had many successes in my career, and I had many good qualities and skills. When I emerged from the bedclothes, I saw that I would never have been promoted if my mentor had not felt that I was a good lawyer. I looked for other examples of what I had accomplished in my career up to that time and understood that I should not depend upon the opinions of others to feel good about myself.

Further, armed with that understanding, I was able to look at my feedback more objectively. My clients weren't unhappy with my *work*; they simply didn't know what I was working on and when to expect results. I then understood what I needed to do to address their concerns. I needed to communicate better with my clients and keep them in the loop!

It seems simple, but there are many attorneys who assume that their clients are clairvoyant and know exactly what is going on in their attorney's office. Although it *feels* like your clients are looking over your shoulder at times, they really don't! I began to take steps to address this, and my performance feedback the next year improved substantially.

While this was a difficult experience, it highlighted that getting this feedback is an important developmental tool. No one had ever been as open and blunt with me before. Attorney managers often feel uncomfortable giving negative feedback to their lawyers, even if it's constructive. Rather, everyone gets into a sort of passive-aggressive loop. The managers/partners get angry because their attorneys aren't performing well; they don't want to criticize them, but often talk about them behind their backs, which reflects badly on the attorneys. The attorneys have no idea what they're doing wrong, so they keep on doing the same thing over and over. Then the managers/partners get angrier because there's no change in the younger attorneys' behavior. Nobody improves; the managers get frustrated and the attorneys get the feeling that "something's wrong," but have no idea why. And then, sometimes, young attorneys lose their jobs or are encouraged to move to another job, where the cycle repeats itself if there is no intervention or awareness.

There are several stages involved in hearing and accepting feedback:

Denial: "They're wrong. I'm a hard worker! I do my job! I'm a good lawyer!"

Anger: "Why are they picking on me? It's the other guy who's screwing up! They're out to get me!"

Depression: "I'll never be good enough! What am I going to do?"

Acceptance: "Okay, even if I disagree, somehow, the clients have this impression of me. I need to look behind the criticism and learn what I need to do to change that impression."

Getting to *acceptance* is the important thing—once you're there, you can address the issues and learn what you need to learn to improve.

And there are resources available to work through this process together with a coach or mentor so you get the most from feedback you receive.

First Step in Finding Your Voice: Exercise

Here is your first step on the path to finding your own true voice. The following is a brief exercise to help you find *your* way to becoming self-aware and self-confident. Find a quiet place and take just fifteen minutes to fill it out. Don't think too hard about any of it. Just go with your first reactions to each question.

Why did you go to law school?

What were your two favorite classes in law school?

What were your two least favorite classes in law school?

What were your two favorite activities as a child?

What are your two favorite activities now?

What are your two best legal skills?

What are your two legal skills that need the most work?

What job do you want to retire from?

What are your two favorite legal activities?

What are your two least favorite legal activities?

What work are you doing in your current legal job?

Go back and look at your favorite and least favorite activities as a child. Which of them are you doing now?

Go back and look at your favorite and least favorite legal activities. Which of them are you doing in your current legal job?

WHAT'S THE NEXT STEP?

Now you should have a better picture of who you are, including your strengths, your weaknesses and your passions. This is the first step in the process of gaining self-knowledge, self-awareness and self-confidence as an attorney.

What's the next step? It often helps to work with someone who can help you see what you might be missing and who can guide you to learn what you need to know in becoming successful as an attorney. A certified professional coach can help you through this process by aiding you to clarify your goals; gain greater self-understanding, leading to increased self-confidence; and hold you accountable for finding your voice and your own unique pathway to success as a lawyer.

A coach can be extremely helpful in assisting you to figure out the root cause of your concerns and find ways to address them in an intentional way. Let's examine a few challenging situations that attorneys find themselves in and observe how a coach can be helpful in dealing with them.

COACHING EXAMPLE #1: "I'VE GOT TOO MUCH TO DO AND TOO LITTLE TIME TO DO IT IN!"

Harry is a second-year associate at a large law firm. He is feeling overwhelmed. He is working fifteen hours a day and every weekend. He has no time for his friends or family. Despite the amount of time he devotes to his work, the partners at his firm have confronted him because he has not finished his assignments on time, nor are they complete. Harry is feeling exhausted, frustrated and confused. One of the partners sees that Harry has a lot of potential as an attorney and is concerned about him. He has observed that Harry has been more productive in the past and sees that Harry is burning himself out without generating results. He suggests that Harry meet with Ann, a certified professional coach, to see if she can help him work more efficiently and effectively. Their first session begins like this:

Ann: Hello, Harry. How can I help you today?

Harry: I'm not sure you can. I'm only meeting with you because the partner forced me to and I really don't have time for this. I just need to work harder...

Ann: Well, Harry, then why do you suppose the partner forced you to meet me?

Harry: I guess it's because I'm not getting my work done on time, and I'm getting criticized all the time for incomplete, late memos. Listen, I really need to get out of here. Can we just say we met, and then I'll get some extra billable hours by going back to the library?

Ann: Harry, I'd really rather concentrate on using the time we have to see what's going on here. What do you feel when you get criticized?

(Harry is reluctant to answer. Attorneys aren't supposed to feel anything — they're just supposed to do their work and be as stoic as possible.)

Ann: Harry, what happens when you don't finish a memo on time?

Harry: It looks like you're not going to give up. Okay, basically, the partner criticizes me, because usually we are on a short timetable and the client's waiting for an answer. Then if it takes me longer to get something done, the client's really irritated and lets the partner know they're unhappy. The partners can sometimes get a little surly...

Ann: Okay, so it sounds to me like that is very difficult for you.

You might be feeling as if you disappointed the partner and maybe that you aren't capable of getting the work done. Does that sound right? *(This is called "acknowledging." The coach recognizes that the partner's behavior is making Harry feel uncomfortable and somewhat degraded. "Acknowledging" is one of the first steps toward establishing a rapport with Harry.)*

Harry: Yeah, I guess that's right. It does really make me feel like an idiot.

Ann: That's totally understandable, Harry. When you've worked hard all the way through law school, passed the bar exam, gotten a good position and labored 24/7 for your firm, and then the partner gets surly with you on top of everything else, it's logical to feel frustrated. *(This process is called "validation." Ann lets Harry know that this reaction to the partner's behavior is normal and justified under the circumstances. It helps Harry feel supported so that he can move past his anger and frustration into a more productive way of working. Demonstrating that Ann has an understanding of how Harry is feeling also begins to establish trust in Ann, a vital part of the coaching relationship.)*

Harry: Thanks. That's true. I thought I was overreacting. I'm just feeling overwhelmed and frustrated because I thought I was doing a good job, and I just can't seem to do everything I am asked to do.

Ann: Sure, Harry. So let me ask you something: Would you like to explore this issue with me so that we can determine what's making you feel that way? *(This is called "asking permission." The coach always asks whether the client would like to commit to looking at what's going on in his or her life before going forward. This way, the client starts to prepare to address his or her issues. It also helps to establish a connection between Ann and Harry.)*

Harry: Well, I guess it couldn't hurt, right? I've already lost most of a billable hour anyway.

Ann: Great, Harry! This is how the process will work. I'm going to ask you some questions, and I'd like you to give them some thought. We can talk about your answers. Then we'll find some ways to help you. So here's my first question: Harry, what is making you feel overwhelmed at work? *(A professional coach will ask many open-ended questions that help the client work toward pinpointing the root cause(s) of the client's issues. Once the client and coach identify the root cause or causes of the issue, the coach will utilize coaching tools to help the client find a way to address them.)*

Harry: I'm just so busy all the time! I have so many assignments, I feel like there just aren't enough hours in the day to finish them! I start one, then a partner comes in and tells me his assignment is more important, so I put one down and pick his up, then another partner comes in and tells me her assignment takes priority and on and on. So I put the other assignment down and pick hers up, and I just can't get ahead, no matter how many hours I stay at the office. I get distracted and I forget where I am on any of them, and then the partners start to tell me that I'm late with the assignments. *(Harry is now feeling more comfortable discussing his feelings and is better able to talk about what's going on with him.)*

Ann: Great, Harry! It's good that you're able to share what's happening with me. This will be very helpful in pinpointing the reasons for the issues and addressing them. *(The coach will also celebrate steps along the way. For example, here,*

Harry, like many attorneys, starts out feeling uncomfortable sharing his feelings or admitting that there is a problem. Taking a step toward opening up about what's going on at the office is important for Ann to acknowledge.)

Ann: So here's the next question, Harry: Why do you suppose you have so many partners asking you to do work for them?

Harry: I guess it's because they *used* to like my work. *(He chuckles a bit.)* Seriously, I think it's partially because I don't turn anyone down. I'm afraid that if I do turn them down, they'll fire me.

Ann: And what makes you think that you would be fired if you turned down work?

Harry *(thinking for a minute)*: It's an employer's market out there. I know how lucky I was to get *this* job. If I turned down work, why would they keep me?

Ann: That's a good question, Harry. Because it seems to me that part of the reason you are taking on so many assignments is your fear. Correct?

Harry: Yes!

Ann: But then you are taking on so many assignments that you aren't able to finish them on time and correctly. Right?

Harry: Yeah, I feel like I'm between a rock and a hard place.

Ann: That's understandable, Harry. Let me ask you this: When you look around at your peers, to what extent are they all feeling the same pressures and fears? To what extent are they also working 24/7 and getting criticized?

Harry: That's a good question, Ann.

I think some of them are and some of them aren't. Some of them seem to be able to balance everything and get into the partners' good graces and never get yelled at by *anyone*. Some are in the same boat with me.

Ann: What do you think the first group does that makes a difference?

Harry: Gosh, Ann. I'm not really sure.

Ann: So some of them aren't afraid, would you say?

Harry: Right. That's true.

Ann: So it sounds to me that to a great extent, your fear is getting in the way of your doing a complete and timely job. And somehow, it appears that some of the other associates have found a way both to say "no" to assignments that will overwhelm them and a way to say "yes" to certain partners to let them know that they enjoy working with particular partners. What do you think?

Harry: I suppose that's at least part of it.

Ann: And by voicing their interest, might they be in a better position to have the partners protect them from work assignments that may be too much for them to do properly and in a timely fashion?

Harry: Yeah, I think that's right.

Ann: Would you like to explore this with me to address your fears and see if we can find your own way to say both "no" *and* "yes," which will let you get better control over your workload?

Harry: Sure. I think that would work.

As you can see, Ann's coaching

process of connecting with Harry and then asking powerful questions to help him identify what is causing his discomfort gives Harry the confidence to find a way to address it. Ann will use additional coaching tools to work with Harry to determine where his fear is coming from, what he can do to address that fear and how he can find his voice in this situation. He will keep busy and get work done without compromising the quality and efficiency of his work.

In Harry's case, Ann sees that there can be many reasons for Harry's situation, including Harry's fear of turning down work, his failure to connect with the partners to understand what's best for the firm under these circumstances and/or his lack of self-confidence that is preventing him from seeking advice and working with the partners to ensure that his work is complete and efficient.

In addition, Harry needs to learn how to express his interest in working for particular partners (i.e., saying "yes") and letting other partners know that he is tied up (i.e., saying "no"). As his coach, she will help him identify his priorities and get to know and appreciate his own strengths. She will then give him some tools to help him find the voice to express himself to the partners to let them know that he really cares about doing a good job. These tools could include observing his peers who seem to be better positioned, and using this knowledge plus his own ideas, planning out how to approach different partners and what he will say to them. This way, he will find the self-confidence to express himself productively so that the partners respect his work and his time.

COACHING EXAMPLE #2: THEY NEVER LISTEN TO ME!!!

Sheila is a third-year associate at a large urban law firm. She enjoys an excellent reputation among the partners as a dogged researcher and diligent document reviewer. The lead partners of her litigation team have now begun to include her in their team meetings. She's finding, however, that whenever she tries to comment and contribute to the discussions, her remarks are ignored. Worse, the other third-year associate on the team, Mark, often repeats her comments and gets praised for his insights! The partners then award Mark with additional responsibilities and developmental opportunities. And Sheila ends up going back to her office to do more legal research and document review. She feels frustrated, defeated and a little angry. A friend of hers recommends that she speak with Ann, a lawyer and certified professional coach. Let's listen as Ann helps Sheila identify the issues involved in this situation and determine what she will need to address in order to find her voice and express herself so she is heard and appreciated:

Ann: Sheila, I'm Ann. I am both an attorney and a certified professional coach. I specialize in helping young attorneys gain confidence and express themselves effectively. *(Ann is disclosing some information about herself, and in so doing, letting Sheila know that she can be trusted. Trust is an essential part of the coaching process — the client must feel comfortable opening up to the coach in order to determine how best to proceed.)* How can I help you today? *(Note that the coach always lets the client set the agenda for the session. Sheila's response will tell Ann where she is in her professional life and better lets Ann know how to help her.)*

Sheila: Hi, Ann. I hope you can help me—I'm pretty frustrated.

Ann: I hope I *can* help you too! What's making you feel frustrated? *(Again, Ann asks an open-ended, powerful question that provokes thought and efficiently lets her know what Sheila needs.)*

Sheila: Well, every time I sit in on a meeting, when I have an idea and I express it, nobody ever seems to hear me. What makes it worse is that Mark, the other third-year associate on the team, waits a minute and then makes *exactly* the same comment. Then the partners all tell him what a great suggestion he's made and he gets all the credit! Then they give him all the good assignments and I end up doing the same old thing over and over again. Plus, I never get the credit for my thoughts! It's *really* annoying!

Ann: Sheila, it sounds like you are trying to contribute to the discussions, you come up with good ideas—as evidenced by the reaction when Mark makes the same comments—and then Mark gets all the credit and recognition. It is totally understandable that you would feel frustrated and maybe a little angry. Is that correct? *(Ann lets Sheila know that she has heard her; she also acknowledges Sheila's concerns and validates her feelings. By mirroring Sheila's response, she demonstrates "active listening," a skill that helps to connect Ann with the client and lets the client know that she has heard her — which is particularly important in this case — and understands the issue.)*

Sheila: Yes, that's exactly right! And the worst part is that they think Mark is some kind of legal genius, and they keep giving him increasing

STRAIGHT TALK FOR LAWYERS

responsibilities. And then they send me back to doing stuff I've been doing since I graduated from law school! It's really annoying!

Ann: Sheila, it sounds as if they are not acknowledging your contributions and, worse, they're crediting Mark for them. It's completely natural to feel frustrated about this kind of thing. *(Ann again acknowledges and validates Sheila's feelings.)* I should tell you that this is something that happens to other people—and they can address it in different ways, depending upon why it's happening. Would you like to work with me to see what we can do to change what's going on with you and perhaps help you be "heard"? *(Here, Ann is "asking permission" to get Sheila's buy-in to work together toward a solution.)*

Sheila *(relieved)*: Yes, I would love to do that! How do we start?

Ann: There are a number of ways to move forward, Sheila. First, let's look at what happens at these meetings, okay? *(As Sheila's coach, Ann needs to understand exactly what is going on at these meetings — somehow, Sheila's voice is not being heard. There can be a number of different explanations for this. For example, Sheila may speak too quietly for the partners to hear her; her voice may be pitched very high and does not carry; her body language may not indicate active involvement in the discussion; she may not know how to capture the attention of the meeting leader; she may not feel confident enough to say, "Hang on, please let me finish my thought.")* Would it be okay for you to close your eyes and imagine yourself at a meeting? *(Again, Ann asks permission to ensure that Sheila is on board with imagining herself at a meeting.)*

Sheila *(closing her eyes)*: Sure, I can do that!

Ann: Okay, please close your eyes and picture yourself at a meeting. Then, please describe the conversation. And please tell me exactly how you are sitting, where you are sitting and who is speaking.

Sheila: So I'm sitting at a round table with about four other people. The lead partner is sitting across from me, and Mark is sitting next to me on my right. There is another partner there next to the lead partner and also two senior associates. The partner asks how we should handle a discovery request from the other side in the litigation. There are a lot of documents to produce, but I've gone through the documents and I have an idea about how to direct the paralegals to review them and prepare them for production really efficiently. I tell the partners about my idea; everyone else is talking, so nobody's listening to *me*. Then about two minutes later, Mark says *exactly* the same thing. The lead partner says, "That's a *great* idea, Mark! How about putting together a team with the paralegals and working on getting that done?" Then he tells me to go back to the document pile, go through the rest of them and get them ready for Mark and *his* team to process and produce!

Ann: Great, Sheila. You can open your eyes now. You did a very good job telling me what happened. Now, I have a few questions for you. What was happening around the table when you made your suggestion?

Sheila: Well, the partner asked the question, and then everybody kind of jumped in to tell him what they thought.

Ann: How were you sitting at the table when you made the suggestion?

Sheila: Gosh, I don't remember. I

may have been sitting back from the table, but I'm not sure.

Ann: Okay, we'll get back to that. In the meantime, see if you can remember what your body position was and how everyone else was sitting. *(This is a coaching technique called "planting the seed," in which Ann poses a question for the client to think about that can help the client come up with potential solutions to his or her dilemma.)* Now, what kind of eye contact was going on around the table?

Sheila: Gee, I'm not sure about that either. I think everyone just jumped in and they were looking at each other. But I guess I should pay attention to that kind of thing.

Ann: You know what? I am with you on that. Let's look at Mark now. In thinking about the meeting, what do you notice about Mark's comment?

Sheila: I think he waited until there was a space in the conversation, like just after everyone else started to talk. I'm not sure what else—maybe he was louder than I was? I don't know.

Ann: That could be. Sheila, as I said before, the kind of interaction you're describing is not unusual, especially for young women or other people who speak quietly. They make a comment at a meeting, nobody hears them and they don't have the confidence to say, "Hey, let me finish my thought." Then they get frustrated because one of their colleagues— sometimes but not always a man—says exactly the same thing and gets praise. So not only was she not heard, she feels as if the male colleague "stole" her idea and then gets the credit. (At times, the coach will "teach" the client about a situation to let the client know that she is in good company and that others have forged a path through the *situation.)* And especially in the United States, our conversation technique is such that people tend to interrupt each other, talk over each other and generally, the loudest voice is the one that's heard.

Sheila: Okay, so I'm not alone, right?

Ann: Right. Also keep in mind that body language, tone of voice and even the cadence of speech can affect how effectively a person communicates. If a person hangs back from the table, she cuts herself off from the group. It can also be helpful to catch the eye of the lead partner, who is the leader of the meeting, to indicate that you have something to say. And a voice that's pitched higher does not carry as readily as one that's pitched lower. Likewise, if a person ends a sentence with an implied question mark, other people think she's asking and not *telling*. So if they're looking for concrete direction, they won't pay attention to what she said. And it's okay to let everyone know that you're speaking and would like to express yourself!

So the first thing we will work on is understanding *how* you communicate in a group setting, which will require you to observe what's happening in the room and in yourself when you speak at a meeting. Do you have any meetings scheduled with this group between now and our next session?

Sheila: Yes, there's one tomorrow.

Ann: Great! So what do you think about doing an assignment between now and our next time together?

Sheila: Sounds good—and it sounds like I should pay attention to what I'm doing at the next meeting, right?

Ann: Yes. Watch what *you're* doing, as well as what Mark does and how he expresses himself. And observe the interactions among the participants. I suggest that you write down everything you observe so that we can discuss it next week. Can you agree to do that? *(Getting agreement on the coaching assignment is extremely important. The client needs to commit to getting this assignment done in order to solve the issue at hand. And only the client can get the assignment done!)*

Sheila: Sure. That sounds good. Is there anything else I should do?

Ann: Yes. One more tool you can use: Prepare for the meeting! Find out what the agenda will be, and do your best to anticipate questions the partners will be asking. That way, when the questions or subjects come up, you won't have to take the time to think about your answer. You can be the "first" to come up with a solution! *(Ann gives Sheila two tools to work with: The first is observational and the second is preparatory.)*

We'll leave Ann and Sheila here. Ann will use additional coaching techniques and skills to work with Sheila to become aware of her style of expressing herself at meetings and find ways to communicate successfully so that the partners hear her voice and recognize her value to the team.

COACHING EXAMPLE #3: WHERE DID ALL MY WORK GO?

Louis is a third-year associate at a midsized law firm on the East Coast. During his first two years at the firm, he kept busy with work and was rewarded with the same raises his peers received. Since the beginning of his third year, however, he began to notice that his workload has diminished. He has always heard that associates should be very busy and that if they start to run out of work, they should start to worry about their job security. Louis asked one of the partners he works with whether he should, indeed, be worried about his job. The partner assured him that everything was "fine" and things were just "slow" because of the economy. She told him to get back to work and not be concerned. But Louis sees that several of his peers are working long hours, even on the weekends, and he's still worried.

In fact, Louis did not Shepardize a case on one of his research assignments. This was a case on which he relied in his memorandum to a partner. The case was overturned the week before the partner's oral argument. The partner was embarrassed at the argument due to this error and was furious with Louis. Notwithstanding, the partner did not give this feedback to Louis. Instead, she blamed him when the subject came up with the other partners. As a result, they stopped giving him work.

Louis knows something is wrong and seeks out Ann, a certified professional coach, to determine what he can do in this situation.

Ann: Hi, Louis. How can I help you today?

Louis: Hi, Ann. I'm really worried about my job. I thought I was doing fine; all of a sudden, my work's dried up. When I talked to the partner I do the most work for, she said everything was fine and not to worry. But all the other associates are really busy and working a lot of hours.

Ann: What's the difference between your hours and their hours?

Louis: Let me put it this way: The sun was still out when I got home last week, and that hasn't happened for at least a year and a half!

Ann: Louis, it sounds as if you're picking up some vibes there, but you can't put your finger on what's happening. In that kind of situation, it's natural to feel worried and concerned. *(Again, Ann is letting Louis know that she's heard him, and she is acknowledging and validating his feelings. This is especially important here as Louis is just getting a "feeling" and hasn't heard anything concrete, so he's doubting himself both substantively and intuitively.)* Would you like to explore this a little more deeply? *(Ann asks permission to go on.)*

Louis: Yes, I really want to get to the bottom of this.

Ann: Great, Louis. So let's go back to the "feedback" that the partner gave you. *(Ann will now help Louis put his feelings in perspective by giving him some information about how many attorneys deal with feedback. Right now, Louis is so overwhelmed with worry and fear that it's difficult for him to see a way out of his predicament.)* You know, lawyers generally have a tough time giving feedback, particularly if it's negative feedback. Why do you suppose that is? *(Here, Ann is helping Louis understand what might be going on for the partner in this situation. This will assist Louis in getting out of his current self-defeating mindset. In this case, even if the situation is irreparable due to the seriousness of Louis' mistake, approaching the partner in a self-confident and self-aware way lets the partner understand he is looking to improve his performance. She will be more likely to be honest with him, so he knows what he is dealing with. And there is the possibility that she will see that he intends to improve and will keep him with the firm. But if he never approaches her, he loses all opportunity to make his own decisions about his future.)*

Louis: Gee, I never thought about that. Well, I guess when you give negative feedback, you need to have thought it through carefully so that you can back up the criticism. Also, I think it might be difficult to deal with the other person's emotions—if you tell someone negative things, they're likely to get upset or angry. Who wants to deal with *that?!*

Ann: Absolutely right! So what do

you think about why the partner hasn't given you specific feedback about your work? What do you think is *really* going on? *(This is an open-ended question designed to help Louis think about his situation and try to put himself in the partner's shoes. This can decrease his feelings of anger and get him into an action-oriented mode in order to solve the issue.)*

Louis: I don't know, Ann. I drafted a memo for this partner who had an oral argument. She lost the argument, and since then she won't give me any work. And I'm not getting much work from any of the partners she works with either.

Ann: What feedback did she give you about the memo?

Louis: Well, at first, she said it was fine. Then she seemed really mad when she came back from the argument. I have a feeling it has something to do with that, but

I don't know what. I suppose I could approach her about it more specifically and find out if I did anything wrong.

Ann: You could do that. It's good to get feedback, even if it's negative. That's really the only way you can learn. How would you ask for that feedback? *(Now Ann is providing Louis with the opportunity to think about and practice how he can address the partner. A basic tenet of the coaching process is that most, if not all, of the answers reside in the client.)*

Louis: I'm not really sure, Ann. I'm afraid that if I approach her, she will just say everything's fine, and then sometime in the not-too-distant future, they'll fire me. I'm just really terrified about my job!

Ann: And where is that fear coming from?

Louis: I suppose she's pretty mad

because she lost the argument. And maybe she blames me and she's emotional about it. I'm still not sure why she would blame me, though. *(Putting himself in the partner's shoes helps Louis get beyond his fear.)*

Ann: Well, we don't know that. But we can talk about what you would do with criticism if the feedback comes back that way. What do you think is the value of getting feedback? *(Ann will explore with Louis his views on feedback and determine with him how he can best ask for it and deal with it.)*

Louis: I think it's pretty important. Around our office, basically, as long as you don't get criticized, you can assume you're doing a good job. But I think it's more that if you don't get criticized *and* you keep getting work, you can assume you're doing a good job. But I'd want to know what I'm doing right so I can keep doing that and what I'm doing wrong so I can avoid *that*.

Ann: So what would you do if you got negative feedback from the partner?

Louis: I think I'd be upset, maybe at her and then maybe at myself. But then I'd try to avoid doing what I did wrong in the past.

Ann: Absolutely! So let's explore this a little more. Would it be okay with you to do a little role-playing? *(Ann is asking permission to use a coaching skill.)*

Louis: I suppose we can try that. What do we do?

Ann: Let's imagine that I am the partner and you are seeking feedback from me.

Louis and Ann use the tool of role-play in order to permit Louis to practice how best to voice his concerns and ask for feedback. He also gets prepared for the "worst," i.e., a performance issue that will compel him to seek another job, as well as the "best," i.e., something that was bad but that he will learn never to do again. Once Louis learns to express himself, at the very least, he will be armed with the pertinent information and can work with Ann to find a better environment in which to practice. It is also possible that the partner will realize that Louis is committed to doing a better job, and she can work with him to coordinate better in the future. She might even admire his being able to express himself to get the feedback he needs to improve his performance.

As we have seen, coaching can be an extremely productive way for attorneys to learn how to express themselves effectively and use their voices to advocate for themselves and their clients.

Call us at Pro Se Coaching, LLC and we can help you move forward, gain confidence and find your true voice as a lawyer!

PRO SE COACHING, LLC

(732) 540-3727

PRO SE, LLC
Coaching for Lawyers
HELPING LAWYERS FIND THEIR VOICE

About Andrea

Andrea L. Colby, Esq. is an attorney and certified professional coach. She specializes in the practice of intellectual property law and her legal experience has taken her from the public to the private and corporate sectors, including over twenty-five years in the intellectual property department of one of the world's largest and most comprehensive health care companies. In addition to her broad experience in the legal field, she has mentored, coached and advised in the areas of management and professional development for attorneys. Andrea received her B.S. in Environmental Engineering from Rensselaer Polytechnic Institute, her J.D. from Albany Law School of Union University, her M.A. in Organizational Management from Fielding Graduate University and her coaching certification through iPEC, the Institute for Professional Excellence in Coaching.

PERSONAL NOTES

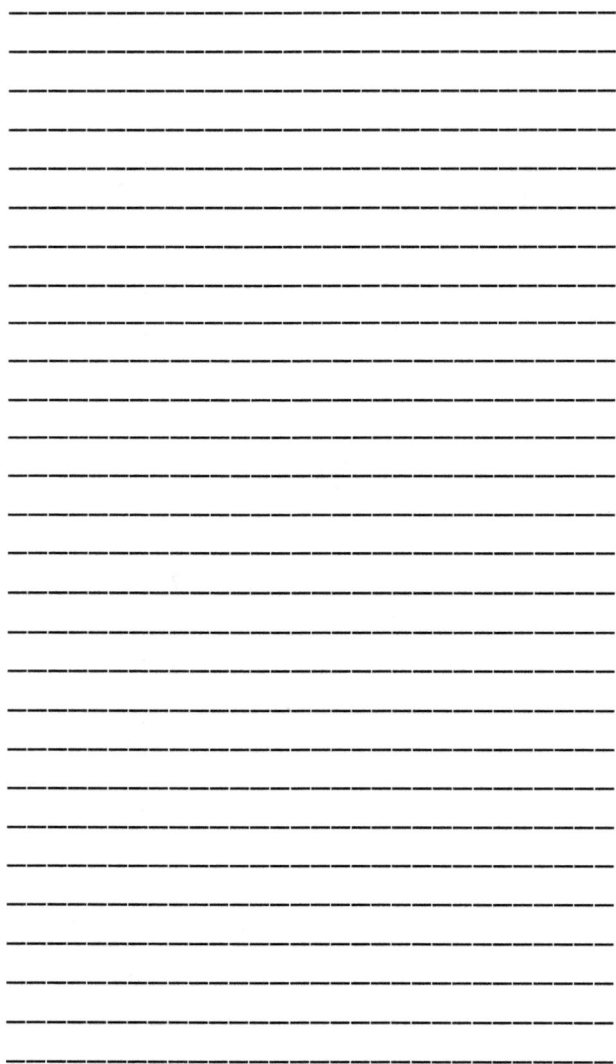

www.ingramcontent.com/pod-product-compliance
Lightning Source LLC
Chambersburg PA
CBHW071014040426
42443CB00007B/763